KB220681

낭독하는 명작동화

Level 3-8

The Little Mermaid

✦·· 인어공주 ··✦

새벽달(남수진) • 이현석 지음

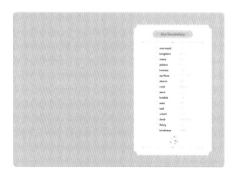

Key Vocabulary

명작동화를 읽기 전에 스토리의 **핵심 단어**를 확인해 보세요. 내가 알고 있는 단어라면 체크 표시하고, 모르는 단어는 이야기를 읽은 후에 체크 표시해 보세요.

Story

Level 3의 영어 텍스트 수준은 책의 난이도를 측정하는 레벨 지수인 **AR(Accelerated Reader) 지수 2.5~3.3 사이**로 **미국 초등학생 2~3학년 수준**으로 맞추고, 분량을 **1100 단어 내외**로 구성했습니다.

쉬운 단어와 간결한 문장으로 구성된 스토리를 그림과 함께 읽어 보세요. 페이지마다 내용 이해를 돕는 그림이 있어 상상력을 풍부하게 해 주며, 이야기를 더욱 재미있게 읽을 수 있습니다.

Reading Training

이현석 선생님의 **강세와 청킹 가이드**에 맞춰 명작동화를 낭독해 보세요.

한국어 번역으로 내용을 확인하고 **우리말 낭독**을 하는 것도 좋습니다.

This Book

Storytelling

명작동화의 내용을 떠올릴 수 있는 **8개의 그림**이 준비되어 있습니다. 각 그림당 제시된 **3개의 단어**를 활용하여 이야기를 만들고 말해 보세요. 상상력과 창의력을 기르는 데 큰 도움이 될 것입니다.

Summary

명작동화의 **줄거리 요약문**이 제시되어 있습니다. 빈칸에 들어갈 단어를 채워 보며 이야기의 내용을 다시 정리해 보세요.

Discussion

명작동화의 내용을 실생활에 응용하거나 비판적으로 생각해 볼 수 있는 **토론 질문**으로 구성했습니다. 영어 또는 우리말로 토론하며 책의 내용을 재구성해 보세요.

픽처 텔링 카드

특별부록으로 **16장의 이야기 그림 카드**가 맨 뒷장에 있어 한 장씩 뜯어서 활용이 가능합니다. 순서에 맞게 그림을 배열하고 이야기 말하기를 해 보세요.

QR코드 영상을 통해 새벽달님과 이현석 선생님이 이 책을 활용하는 가장 좋은 방법을 직접 설명해 드립니다!

Contents

The Little Mermaid

◆╟• 인어공주 •╢◆

- ☐ **mermaid**   인어
- ☐ **kingdom**   왕국
- ☐ **voice**   목소리
- ☐ **palace**   궁전
- ☐ **human**   인간
- ☐ **surface**   수면; 표면
- ☐ **storm**   폭풍
- ☐ **rock**   뒤흔들다
- ☐ **save**   구하다
- ☐ **bubble**   거품
- ☐ **soul**   영혼
- ☐ **tail**   꼬리
- ☐ **witch**   마녀
- ☐ **deck**   (배의) 갑판
- ☐ **fairy**   요정
- ☐ **kindness**   친절함

Once upon a time, there was a little mermaid.

She lived in a kingdom deep underwater.

She was a princess with five older sisters.

She was the youngest.

So everyone called her The Little Mermaid.

The Little Mermaid had a beautiful voice.

She lived in a beautiful palace.

It was made of bright coral and shells.

The palace had a big garden with flowers.

The sea animals were friends of the Little Mermaid.

The Little Mermaid liked to spend time with her grandmother.
Sometimes, the grandmother told her stories about humans.
The Little Mermaid loved those stories.
She wanted to go and see the human world.
But she could not go yet.
She had to wait until she turned fifteen.

The Little Mermaid's sisters had seen the human world.

They came back with exciting stories.

"I saw ships and towns," said one sister.

"I saw birds and big clouds," said another.

"What is a bird?" the Little Mermaid asked.

"They are fish on trees," the sister answered.

The Little Mermaid wanted to see more.

Finally, the Little Mermaid turned fifteen.
She was very happy and excited.
She quickly swam up to the surface.
The sky was beautiful and blue.
Then, she saw a big ship with many people.

There was a party for the prince's birthday.
The prince had kind eyes and a beautiful smile.
The Little Mermaid watched him from the water.
She fell in love with him at first sight.

Suddenly, there was a big storm.
The wind was strong and wild.
The waves rocked the ship left and right.

The ship started to break, and people fell into the sea.
The Little Mermaid looked for the prince.
'He should not die,' she thought.

The Little Mermaid found the prince in the water.
She hugged him and took him to the beach.
She saved him from the storm.

The prince was alive, but he was asleep.
The Little Mermaid stayed beside the prince.
The prince did not know she was there.

Then, a human princess walked by.
The Little Mermaid quickly hid behind a rock.
The human princess called other people for help.

The prince opened his eyes.
He could only see the human princess.
"Thank you for saving my life," said the prince.

The Little Mermaid saw everything.
And she dived back into the sea.
Back at the palace, she wanted to see the prince again.
She thought about him every day.
She wanted him to love her.
But she was a mermaid, and he was a human.

The Little Mermaid asked many questions to her grandmother.

"Grandmother, how long do humans live?" she asked.

"We mermaids live for three hundred years.

And then we turn into bubbles.

But humans live only for eighty or ninety years.

Then, their souls go up to the sky. Their souls stay there forever."

The Little Mermaid wanted a human soul.

She wanted to live with the prince.

She also wanted to walk on land.

Her tail was beautiful, but she wanted to walk with her feet.

The Little Mermaid's sisters saw their youngest sister.
"What is wrong, sister?" one of them asked.
"Nothing," the Little Mermaid answered.
She could not tell them about the prince.

She often went above the water.
Sometimes, she saw the prince in the castle.
He seemed to have a happy life with his family and friends.

One day, the Little Mermaid went to the sea witch.
'Maybe she can turn me into a human,' she thought.
The sea witch was scary and powerful.
She lived in a dark cave.

The sea witch knew the Little Mermaid's wish.
"I can make special water. This water will give you legs.
But the prince must marry you.
If he does not, you will die," said the witch.

The Little Mermaid was scared.

"Okay, give me the water," she said.

"Also, I want your voice," said the witch.

The Little Mermaid thought for a while.

She loved to sing with her beautiful voice.

She hesitated, then finally said, "Take my voice."

So, the witch gave her the magic water.

The Little Mermaid drank it.

The next morning, the Little Mermaid opened her eyes.

She was near the prince's castle.

She had two human legs, but she felt great pain.

The prince found her on the beach.

'Maybe this girl hurt her legs,' he thought.

He took care of her in the castle.

They spent many days together.

The Little Mermaid wanted to talk to the prince.

But without her voice, she could not talk to him.

The prince did not know the Little Mermaid had saved him.
He thought it was the human princess who had saved him.
'She is not the one who saved you! It was me!'
the Little Mermaid spoke with her eyes.

The Little Mermaid was sad.
But she always stayed with the prince.
She hoped he would love her.

One day, the prince decided to marry the human princess.
The Little Mermaid was heartbroken.
She wanted to tell him the truth.

The day of the wedding came.
There was a big celebration on a ship.
Everyone was happy except for the Little Mermaid.
She knew it was the day of her death.
The prince and the human princess got married.
'I will die before morning comes,' the Little Mermaid thought.

That night, the Little Mermaid was looking at the sea.

She saw bubbles on the water.

'What is that?' she thought.

It was her sisters who came to find her!

"Sister! We know everything now. Please do not die,"
the sisters cried.

"We know a way to save you," they said.

"Kill the prince with this knife. Then you can live."

One sister threw the knife onto the ship.

The Little Mermaid thought for a long time.

She did not want to kill the prince.

But she also did not want to die.

The Little Mermaid held the knife.
She went to the prince's room.
She looked at the sleeping prince.
She loved him, so she could not kill him.

The Little Mermaid went out to the deck again.
Then she threw the knife into the sea.
The water around the knife turned red.
She decided to leave the prince.

The Little Mermaid jumped into the sea.
But she could not swim because she did not have a tail.
She sank deep into the water.

Morning came, but the Little Mermaid was still alive.
And her tail was back. She was surprised.
'I did not turn into bubbles!' she thought.

Then, something magical happened.
A fairy appeared and said to her, "I am the fairy of air.
If you show kindness, you can have a soul.
And you can live forever."

The Little Mermaid suffered, but she showed kindness.
So, as the fairy of air said, her soul went up to the sky.
And she lived forever.

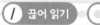
◆ The Little Mermaid

Once upon a **ti**me, **/** there was a **lit**tle **mer**maid.
She **li**ved in a **king**dom **/** **deep** under**wa**ter.
She was a **prin**cess **/** with **fi**ve **old**er **sis**ters.
She was the **young**est.
So **e**veryone **call**ed her **/** The **Lit**tle **Mer**maid.
The **Lit**tle **Mer**maid **/** **had** a **beau**tiful **voi**ce.

She **li**ved **/** in a **beau**tiful **pa**lace.
It was **ma**de of **/** **bright co**ral and **shells**.
The **pa**lace **/** **had** a **big gar**den **/** with **flo**wers.
The **sea a**nimals **/** were **fri**ends of the **Lit**tle **Mer**maid.

The **Lit**tle **Mer**maid **/** **li**ked to **spend ti**me **/** with her **grand**mother.
Sometimes, **/** the **grand**mother **told** her **sto**ries **/** about **hu**mans.
The **Lit**tle **Mer**maid **/** **lo**ved those **sto**ries.
She **want**ed to **/** **go** and **see** the **hu**man **world**.
But she could **not** **/** **go** yet.
She **had** to **wait** **/** until she **turn**ed fif**teen**.

◆ 인어공주

옛날 옛날에, 어린 인어가 있었습니다.
그녀는 깊은 바닷속 왕국에서 살았어요.
그녀는 다섯 명의 언니가 있는 공주였습니다.
그녀가 막내였어요.
그래서 모두가 그녀를 인어공주라고 불렀답니다.
인어공주는 아름다운 목소리를 가지고 있었어요.

그녀는 아름다운 궁전에서 살았습니다.
궁전은 밝은 빛 산호와 조개껍데기로 만들어져 있었어요.
궁전에는 꽃들이 가득한 커다란 정원도 있었습니다.
바다 동물들이 인어공주의 친구였어요.

인어공주는 할머니와 시간을 보내는 것을 좋아했어요.
때때로, 할머니는 인어공주에게 인간들에 대한 이야기를 들려주었어요.
인어공주는 그 이야기를 아주 좋아했습니다.
그녀는 인간 세상을 보러 가고 싶었어요.
하지만 그녀는 아직 갈 수 없었습니다.
그녀는 열다섯 살이 될 때까지 기다려야 했어요.

The **Lit**tle **Mer**maid's **sis**ters had **seen** / the **hu**man **world**.

They came **back** / with ex**ci**ting **sto**ries.

"I **saw ships** and **towns**," / said one **sis**ter.

"I **saw birds** / and **big clouds**," / said another.

"**What** is a **bird**?" / the **Lit**tle **Mer**maid asked.

"They are **fish** on **trees**," / the **sis**ter answered.

The **Lit**tle **Mer**maid / **want**ed to **see mo**re.

Finally, / the **Lit**tle **Mer**maid / **turn**ed fif**teen**.

She was **ve**ry **hap**py / and ex**ci**ted.

She **quick**ly swam **up** / to the **sur**face.

The **sky** was **beau**tiful / and **blue**.

Then, / she **saw** a **big ship** / with **ma**ny **peo**ple.

There was a **par**ty / for the **prin**ce's **birth**day.

The **prin**ce / **had kind eyes** / and a **beau**tiful **smi**le.

The **Lit**tle **Mer**maid **watch**ed him / from the **wa**ter.

She **fell** in **lo**ve with him / at **first sight**.

인어공주의 언니들은 인간 세상을 본 적이 있었습니다.
언니들은 흥미진진한 이야기를 가지고 돌아왔어요.
"나는 배와 마을을 봤어." 한 언니가 말했습니다.
"나는 새들과 커다란 구름을 보았어." 다른 언니가 말했어요.
"새가 뭐야?" 인어공주가 물었습니다.
"새는 나무에 사는 물고기야." 언니가 대답했어요.
인어공주는 더 많은 것들을 보고 싶었습니다.

마침내, 인어공주가 열다섯 살이 되었습니다.
그녀는 매우 행복하고 신이 났어요.
그녀는 빠르게 수면으로 헤엄쳐 올라갔습니다.
하늘은 아름답고 푸르렀어요.
그때, 그녀는 많은 사람들을 태운 큰 배 한 척을 보았습니다.

그곳에서는 왕자의 생일 파티가 열리고 있었습니다.
왕자는 친절한 눈과 아름다운 미소를 가지고 있었어요.
인어공주는 물속에서 그를 바라보았습니다.
그녀는 첫눈에 그와 사랑에 빠졌습니다.

Suddenly, **/** there was a **big storm**.

The **wind** was **strong** **/** and **wild**.

The **waves** **/** **rock**ed the **ship** **/** **left** and **right**.

The **ship start**ed to **break**, **/** and **peo**ple **/** **fell** into the **sea**.

The **Lit**tle **Mer**maid **/** **look**ed for the **prin**ce.

'He should **not die**,' **/** she thought.

The **Lit**tle **Mer**maid **/** **found** the **prin**ce in the **wa**ter.

She **hug**ged him **/** and **took** him **/** to the **beach**.

She **sa**ved him **/** from the **storm**.

The **prin**ce was a**li**ve, **/** but he was a**sleep**.

The **Lit**tle **Mer**maid **/** **stay**ed be**si**de the **prin**ce.

The **prin**ce did **not know** **/** she was **there**.

Then, **/** a **hu**man **prin**cess **/** walked **by**.

The **Lit**tle **Mer**maid **quick**ly **/** **hid** behind a **rock**.

The **hu**man **prin**cess **/** **call**ed **o**ther **peo**ple for **help**.

갑자기, 커다란 폭풍이 몰아쳤습니다.
바람은 강하고 사나웠어요.
파도가 배를 이리저리 흔들었습니다.

배가 부서지기 시작했고, 사람들이 바다에 빠졌습니다.
인어공주는 왕자를 찾아 헤맸어요.
'그는 죽으면 안 돼.' 인어공주는 생각했어요.

인어공주는 물속에서 왕자를 발견했습니다.
그녀는 그를 안고 해변으로 데려갔어요.
그녀는 그를 폭풍으로부터 구해 냈습니다.

왕자는 살아났지만, 잠들어 있었습니다.
인어공주는 왕자의 곁을 지켰어요.
왕자는 그녀가 곁에 있는 것을 알지 못했습니다.

그때, 한 인간 공주가 지나갔습니다.
인어공주는 재빨리 바위 뒤로 숨었어요.
인간 공주는 다른 사람들을 불러 도움을 청했습니다.

The **prin**ce / **o**pened his **eyes**.

He could **on**ly **see** / the **hu**man **prin**cess.

"**Thank** you / for **sa**ving my **life**," / said the **prin**ce.

The **Lit**tle **Mer**maid / **saw e**verything.

And she **di**ved / **back** into the **sea**.

Back at the **pa**lace, / she **want**ed to **see** the **prin**ce a**gain**.

She **thought** about him / every **day**.

She **want**ed him / to **lo**ve her.

But she was a **mer**maid, / and he was a **hu**man.

The **Lit**tle **Mer**maid / **ask**ed **ma**ny **ques**tions / to her **grand**mother.

"**Grand**mother, / **how** long do **hu**mans **li**ve?" / she asked.

"**We mer**maids / **li**ve for **three** hundred **years**.

And then we **turn** into **bub**bles.

But **hu**mans / **li**ve **on**ly for **eighty** / or **ni**nety **years**.

Then, / their **souls** / go **up** to the **sky**.

Their **souls** stay there for**ev**er."

왕자가 두 눈을 떴어요.
그는 인간 공주만을 볼 수 있었습니다.
"제 목숨을 구해 주셔서 고마워요." 왕자가 말했어요.

인어공주는 모든 것을 지켜보았습니다.
그리고 다시 바다로 뛰어들었습니다.
궁전으로 돌아온 인어공주는 다시 왕자가 보고 싶었어요.
그녀는 매일 그를 생각했어요.
그녀는 왕자가 자신을 사랑해 주기를 원했습니다.
하지만 그녀는 인어였고, 그는 인간이었어요.

인어공주는 할머니에게 많은 질문을 했습니다.
"할머니, 인간들은 얼마나 오래 살죠?" 그녀가 물었습니다.
"우리 인어들은 삼백 년을 살지.
그리고 우리는 물거품으로 변한단다.
하지만 인간들은 겨우 팔십 년이나 구십 년을 살아.
그러고 나서, 그들의 영혼은 하늘로 올라간단다.
인간들의 영혼은 하늘에 영원히 머물지."

The **Lit**tle **Mer**maid **/ want**ed a **hu**man **soul**.

She **want**ed to **live / with the **prin**ce.

She **al**so **want**ed to **/ walk** on **land**.

Her **tail** was **beau**tiful, **/ but she **want**ed to **walk / with her **feet**.

The **Lit**tle **Mer**maid's **sis**ters **/ saw their **young**est **sis**ter.

"**What** is **wrong**, **sis**ter?" **/ one** of them asked.

"**No**thing," **/ the **Lit**tle **Mer**maid answered.

She could **not tell** them **/ about the **prin**ce.

She **of**ten **went / a**bove the **wa**ter.

Sometimes, **/ she **saw** the **prin**ce **/ in the **cas**tle.

He **seem**ed to have a **hap**py life **/ with his **fa**mily and **fri**ends.

One day, **/ the **Lit**tle **Mer**maid **/ went** to the **sea witch**.

'**May**be she can **turn** me **/ into a **hu**man,' **/ she thought.

The **sea witch / was **sca**ry and **po**werful.

She **li**ved **/ in a **dark ca**ve.

인어공주는 인간의 영혼을 갖고 싶었습니다.
그리고 왕자와 함께 살고 싶었어요.
그녀는 또한 땅 위를 걷고 싶었습니다.
그녀의 꼬리 지느러미는 아름다웠지만, 그녀는 두 발로 걷고 싶었어요.

인어공주의 언니들이 막냇동생을 보았습니다.
"무슨 일이 있니, 동생아?" 한 언니가 물었어요.
"아무 일도 아니야." 인어공주가 대답했습니다.
그녀는 언니들에게 왕자에 대해 이야기할 수 없었어요.

그녀는 자주 물 위로 올라갔습니다.
가끔, 그녀는 성에 있는 왕자를 보았어요.
그는 가족과 친구들과 함께 행복한 삶을 사는 것 같았습니다.

어느 날, 인어공주는 바다 마녀를 찾아갔습니다.
'어쩌면 마녀가 나를 인간으로 변하게 할 수 있을지도 몰라.' 인어공주가 생각했어요.
바다 마녀는 무섭고 강력했습니다.
그녀는 어두운 동굴에서 살았어요.

The **sea witch** / **knew** the **Lit**tle **Mer**maid's **wish**.

"I can **ma**ke / **spe**cial **wa**ter.

This water / will **gi**ve you **legs**.

But the **prin**ce / **must mar**ry you.

If he does **not**, / you will **die**," / said the **witch**.

The **Lit**tle **Mer**maid / was **scar**ed.

"O**kay**, / **gi**ve me the **wa**ter," / she said.

"**Al**so, / I **want** your **voi**ce," / said the **witch**.

The **Lit**tle **Mer**maid / **thought** for a **while**.

She **lo**ved to **sing** / with her **beau**tiful **voi**ce.

She **he**sitated, / then **fi**nally said, / "**Ta**ke my **voi**ce."

So, the **witch** / **ga**ve her the **ma**gic **wa**ter.

The **Lit**tle **Mer**maid / **drank** it.

The **next mor**ning, / the **Lit**tle **Mer**maid **o**pened her **eyes**.

She was near the **prin**ce's **cas**tle.

She had **two** human **legs**, / but she **felt great pain**.

바다 마녀는 인어공주의 소원을 알고 있었습니다.
"나는 특별한 물약을 만들 수 있지.
이 물약이 너에게 두 다리를 줄 거야.
하지만 왕자가 너와 결혼해야만 해.
그렇지 않으면, 너는 죽을 거야." 마녀가 말했습니다.

인어공주는 무서웠어요.
"알았어요, 저에게 물약을 주세요." 인어공주가 말했습니다.
"그리고 또, 나는 네 목소리가 갖고 싶어." 마녀가 말했어요.
인어공주는 잠시 생각했습니다.
그녀는 자신의 아름다운 목소리로 노래하는 것을 아주 좋아했거든요.
인어공주는 망설이다가, 마침내 말했습니다. "제 목소리를 가져가세요."
그래서, 마녀는 인어공주에게 마법의 물약을 주었습니다.
인어공주는 물약을 마셨습니다.

다음 날 아침, 인어공주는 두 눈을 떴습니다.
그녀는 왕자의 성 근처에 있었어요.
그녀는 두 개의 인간 다리를 가지고 있었지만, 큰 고통을 느꼈습니다.

The **prin**ce **found** her / on the **beach**.

'**May**be this **girl** / **hurt** her **legs**,' / he thought.

He **took ca**re of her / in the **cas**tle.

They **spent ma**ny **days** / to**ge**ther.

The **Lit**tle **Mer**maid / **want**ed to **talk** to the **prin**ce.

But with**out** her **voi**ce, / she could **not talk** to him.

The **pri**nce did **not know** / the **Lit**tle **Mer**maid had **sa**ved him.

He **thought** / it was the **hu**man **prin**cess / who had **sa**ved him.

'She is **not** the **one** / who **sa**ved you!

It was **me**!' / the **Lit**tle **Mer**maid / **spo**ke with her **eyes**.

The **Lit**tle **Mer**maid was **sad**.

But she **al**ways / **stay**ed with the **prin**ce.

She **ho**ped / he would **lo**ve her.

One day, / the **prin**ce de**ci**ded to **mar**ry / the **hu**man **prin**cess.

The **Lit**tle **Mer**maid / was **heart**broken.

She **want**ed to **tell** him / the **truth**.

왕자가 그녀를 해변에서 발견했습니다.

'이 소녀는 다리를 다친 모양이군.' 왕자는 생각했어요.

그는 성에서 인어공주를 보살폈습니다.

그들은 여러 날들을 함께 보냈어요.

인어공주는 왕자에게 이야기하고 싶었습니다.

하지만 그녀는 목소리를 낼 수 없어 그에게 아무 말도 할 수 없었습니다.

왕자는 인어공주가 자신을 구했다는 사실을 몰랐습니다.

그는 자신을 구한 것이 인간 공주라고 생각했지요.

'당신을 구한 건 그녀가 아니에요!

그건 저였어요!' 인어공주는 두 눈으로 말했습니다.

인어공주는 슬펐습니다.

하지만 그녀는 항상 왕자 곁에 머물렀어요.

그녀는 그가 자신을 사랑해 주기를 바랐습니다.

어느 날, 왕자는 인간 공주와 결혼하기로 마음먹었습니다.

인어공주는 가슴이 아팠어요.

그녀는 그에게 진실을 말하고 싶었습니다.

The **day** of the **wed**ding **/ ca**me.

There was a **big** cele**bra**tion **/** on a **ship**.

Everyone was **hap**py **/** ex**cept** for the **Lit**tle **Mer**maid.

She **knew /** it was the **day** of her **death**.

The **prin**ce and the **hu**man **prin**cess **/** got **mar**ried.

'I will **die /** before **mor**ning **co**mes,' **/** the **Lit**tle **Mer**maid thought.

That night, **/** the **Lit**tle **Mer**maid **/** was **look**ing at the **sea**.

She **saw bub**bles **/** on the **wa**ter.

'**What** is **that**?' **/** she thought.

It was her **sis**ters **/** who **ca**me to **find** her!

"**Sis**ter! **/** We **know e**verything **now**.

Please do **not** die," **/** the **sis**ters cried.

"We **know** a **way /** to **sa**ve you," **/** they said.

"**Kill** the **prin**ce **/** with this **knif**e. **/ Then /** you can **li**ve."

One sister **/ threw** the **knif**e **/** onto the **ship**.

The **Lit**tle **Mer**maid **/ thought** for a **long ti**me.

She did **not / want** to **kill** the **prin**ce.

But she **al**so did **not / want** to **die**.

The **Lit**tle **Mer**maid **/ held** the **knif**e.

She **went** to the **prin**ce's **room**.

She **look**ed at the **sleep**ing **prin**ce.

She **lo**ved him, **/** so she could **not kill** him.

결혼식 날이 다가왔습니다.
배 위에서 성대한 축하 행사가 열렸어요.
모두가 행복했지만 인어공주만은 그렇지 않았어요.
그녀는 오늘이 자신이 죽는 날이라는 사실을 알고 있었습니다.
왕자와 인간 공주는 결혼했습니다.
'아침이 오기 전에 나는 죽겠지.' 인어공주가 생각했어요.

그날 밤, 인어공주는 바다를 바라보고 있었습니다.
그녀는 물 위에 떠 있는 물거품을 보았어요.
'저게 뭐지?' 인어공주가 생각했습니다.
바로 인어공주를 찾으러 온 그녀의 언니들이었어요!

"동생아! 이제 우리도 모든 것을 알아.
부디 죽지 마." 언니들이 외쳤습니다.
"우리가 너를 구할 방법을 알아." 언니들이 말했어요.
"이 칼로 왕자를 죽여. 그러면 너는 살 수 있어."
언니 한 명이 칼을 배 위로 던졌습니다.
인어공주는 오랫동안 고민했어요.
그녀는 왕자를 죽이고 싶지 않았습니다.
하지만 그녀는 죽고 싶지도 않았어요.

인어공주는 칼을 꼭 붙들었습니다.
그녀는 왕자의 방으로 갔어요.
그녀는 자고 있는 왕자를 바라보았습니다.
그녀는 그를 사랑했기 때문에 죽일 수 없었어요.

The **Lit**tle **Mer**maid **/** went **out /** to the **deck** a**gain**.
Then she **threw** the **kni**fe **/** into the **sea**.
The **wa**ter around the **knife /** turned **red**.
She de**ci**ded to **/ leave** the **prin**ce.

The **Lit**tle **Mer**maid **jump**ed **/** into the **sea**.
But she could **not swim /** because she did **not /** have a **tail**.
She **sank deep /** into the **wa**ter.

Morning **ca**me, **/** but the **Lit**tle **Mer**maid **/** was **still** a**li**ve.
And her **tail** was **back**. **/** She was sur**pri**sed.
'I did **not turn /** into **bub**bles!' **/** she thought.

Then, **/ so**mething **ma**gical **hap**pened.
A **fai**ry **/** ap**pear**ed and said to her, **/** "I am the **fai**ry of **air**.
If you **show kind**ness, **/** you can **have** a **soul**.
And you can **li**ve for**e**ver."

The **Lit**tle **Mer**maid **suf**fered, **/** but she **show**ed **kind**ness.
So, **/** as the **fai**ry of **air** said, **/** her **soul** went **up** to the **sky**.
And she **li**ved **/** for**e**ver.

인어공주는 다시 갑판으로 나갔습니다.
그리고는 칼을 바다로 던졌어요.
칼 주위의 바닷물이 붉게 변했습니다.
그녀는 왕자를 떠나기로 결심했어요.

인어공주는 바다로 뛰어들었습니다.
하지만 그녀는 꼬리 지느러미가 없었기 때문에 수영을 할 수 없었어요.
그녀는 바다로 깊이 가라앉았습니다.

아침이 되었지만, 인어공주는 여전히 살아 있었습니다.
그리고 그녀의 꼬리 지느러미가 돌아왔어요. 인어공주는 놀랐어요.
'나는 물거품으로 변하지 않았어!' 그녀가 말했습니다.

그때, 마법 같은 일이 일어났습니다.
한 요정이 나타나서 그녀에게 말했어요. "저는 공기의 요정이에요.
친절을 베풀면 영혼을 가질 수 있답니다.
이제 당신은 영원히 살 수 있어요."

인어공주는 고통을 겪었지만, 친절함을 보여 주었어요.
그래서, 공기의 요정이 말한 대로, 그녀의 영혼은 하늘로 올라갔어요.
그리고 그녀는 영원히 살게 되었답니다.

Storytelling

Part 1 ◆ p.8~18

mermaid, palace, human

fifteen, surface, party

storm, prince, save

witch, voice, drink

legs, talk, sad

truth, wedding, death

knife, leave, jump

alive, fairy, soul

voice   kill   kingdom   soul   married

Once upon a time, the Little Mermaid lived in an underwater

_____ with her family. She loved hearing stories about

humans and wanted to see their world. When she turned fifteen, she

saw a human prince and saved him from a storm. To be with him, the

Little Mermaid visited a sea witch. She traded her _____

for human legs. The Little Mermaid and the prince met again. He

took care of her, but he did not know that she saved him. In the end,

the prince _____ another princess. The Little Mermaid

faced death, but she could not _____ him to save herself.

She jumped into the sea, but she was still alive. The Little Mermaid's

kindness allowed her to live forever with a _____ .

Memo

Discussion

1 ◆ (If you are a parent, please be prepared with your own response in case your child cannot think of an answer.) The Little Mermaid was willing to give up her beautiful voice to become a human. Have you ever had to give up something important to you, so that you could get what you wanted? Can you share that experience?

(여러분이 부모라면, 아이가 대답을 생각하지 못할 수 있으니 여러분의 경험을 미리 생각해 두었다가 들려주세요.) 인어공주는 인간이 되기 위해서 자신의 아름다운 목소리를 기꺼이 포기했어요. 여러분도 원하는 무언가를 얻기 위해 소중한 것을 포기해야 했던 경험이 있나요? 그 경험에 대해 말해 줄 수 있나요?

2 ◆ The Little Mermaid saved the prince, but he did not know she was the one who saved him. Was there a situation where you helped someone, but they did not know that you helped them? How did you feel then? What do you think you should do in such a situation?

인어공주는 왕자를 구했지만, 왕자는 자신을 구한 사람이 그녀라는 것을 알지 못했어요. 여러분도 누군가를 도왔지만, 그 사람은 여러분의 도움을 받았다는 사실을 몰랐던 경우가 있었나요? 그때 어떤 기분이었나요? 그런 상황에서는 어떻게 해야 할까요?

낭독하는 명작동화 **Level 3-8**
The Little Mermaid

초판 1쇄 발행 2024년 12월 2일

지은이 새벽달(남수진) 이현석 롱테일 교육 연구소
책임편집 강지희 | **편집** 명채린 백지연 홍하늘
디자인 박새롬 | **그림** 김진우
마케팅 두잉글 사업본부

펴낸이 이수영
펴낸곳 롱테일북스
출판등록 제2015-000191호
주소 04033 서울특별시 마포구 양화로 113, 3층(서교동, 순흥빌딩)
전자메일 team@ltinc.net

이 도서는 대한민국에서 제작되었습니다.
롱테일북스는 롱테일㈜의 출판 브랜드입니다.

ISBN 979-11-93992-32-6 14740

The Little Mermaid

6

questions
years
soul

새벽달 X 이현석 낭독스쿨

The Little Mermaid

5

human
hide
open

새벽달 X 이현석 낭독스쿨

The Little Mermaid

8

witch
human
legs

새벽달 X 이현석 낭독스쿨

The Little Mermaid

7

water
prince
castle

새벽달 X 이현석 낭독스쿨